Mummies

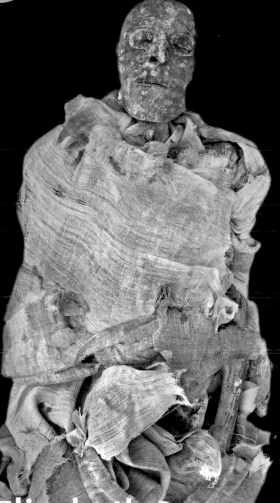

Elizabeth Carney

NATIONAL GEOGRAPHIC
Washington, D.C.

For Patrick, Brendan, Brian, and Nora. Unlike mummies, laughing with you never gets old.—E.C.

Library of Congress Cataloging-in-Publication Data

Carney, Elizabeth, 1981-
Mummies / by Elizabeth Carney.
p. cm.
ISBN 978-1-4263-0528-3 (pbk. : alk. paper) -- ISBN 978-1-4263-0529-0 (library binding : alk. paper)
1. Mummies--Juvenile literature. I. Title.
GN293.C37 2009
393'.3--dc22
2009003630

Printed in the United States of America
09/WOR/1

Cover: © Todd Gipstein/ National Museum, Lima, Peru/ NationalGeographicStock.com; 1, 32 (middle, right): © DEA/ S. Vannini/ DeAgostini Picture Library/ Getty Images; 2: © ancientnile/ Alamy; 5 (both): © Christina Gascoigne/ Robert Harding Picture Library Ltd./ Alamy; 6: © Marwan Naamani/ AFP/ Getty Images; 7: © O. Louis Mazzatenta/ NationalGeographicStock.com; 8: © British Museum/ Art Resource, NY; 9, 32 (middle, left): © Glen Allison/ Photographer's Choice/ Getty Images; 10-11: © Robin Weaver/ Alamy; 12: © Vienna Report Agency/ Sygma/ Corbis; 13: © MARKA/ Alamy; 14-15: © Marc DeVille/ Getty Images; 16: © South American Pictures: 17: © Enrico Ferorelli; 18-19: © Illustration by Kimberly Schamber; 20: © Kenneth Garrett/ National Geographic/ Getty Images; 21: © AP Photo/ Ric Francis; 22: © Time Life Pictures/ Getty Images; 23 (top): © Robert Harding World Imagery/ Getty Images; 23 (right): © Stapleton Collection/ Corbis; 24: © Erich Lessing/ British Museum/ Art Resource, NY; 25 (top): © Alistair Duncan/ Dorling Kindersley/ Getty Images; 25 (bottom): © Carl & Ann Purcell/ Corbis; 26, 27: © Hunan Provincial Museum; 29, 32 (bottom, left): © University College Museum, London, UK/ The Bridgeman Art Library; 30, 31: © Ira Block/ NationalGeographicStock.com; 32 (top, left): © Shutterstock; 32 (top, right): © Dr. Fred Hossler/ Visuals Unlimited/ Getty Images; 32 (bottom, right): © Bojan Brecelj/ Corbis.

Table of Contents

Whoa, Mummy!

A farmer is working in
swampy land. His shovel hits
something hard. He uncovers
a blackened body.

It has hair, teeth, even fingerprints.
The farmer calls the police.
It looks like the person died recently.
But the body is over two thousand
years old! It's a mummy!

The Grauballe Man, found in a swampy bog

Mummy Making

When something dies, it decays. Insects, wild animals, and bacteria eat parts of the body.

A mummy is
a dead body that
doesn't decay.

A mummy can be
made in two ways.

People can use
bacteria-killing
chemicals to
make mummies.

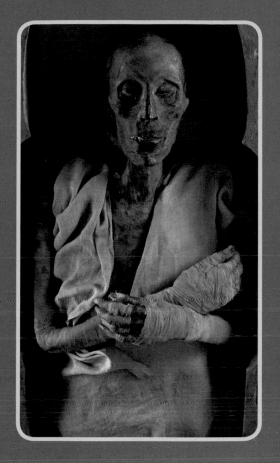

Or, if a body is in the
right place at the right
time, it can also become
a mummy naturally.
In those places, any
dead body might
become a mummy!

BACTERIA: Tiny living
things that can only
be seen through a
microscope.

DECAY: To rot or
break down.

Natural Mummies

A bog mummy known as
the Lindow Man

Body-eating bacteria do not grow well in places that are very cold. Or in places that are hot and dry. Or in places called bogs. People have found mummies on frosty mountaintops and in hot deserts.

Bogs are wet, swamp-like places. Bog mummies can be so well kept that scientists could tell one ancient man used hair gel!

BOGS: Swampy areas where special mosses grow. The plants make the area a tough place for bacteria to live.

The man's face looks like he's sleeping. But he didn't die peacefully.

This bog mummy in Denmark was found with a rope around his neck. Experts think the man was killed as part of a religious ceremony.

The bits of his last meal, vegetable soup eaten 2,300 years ago, are still in his stomach.

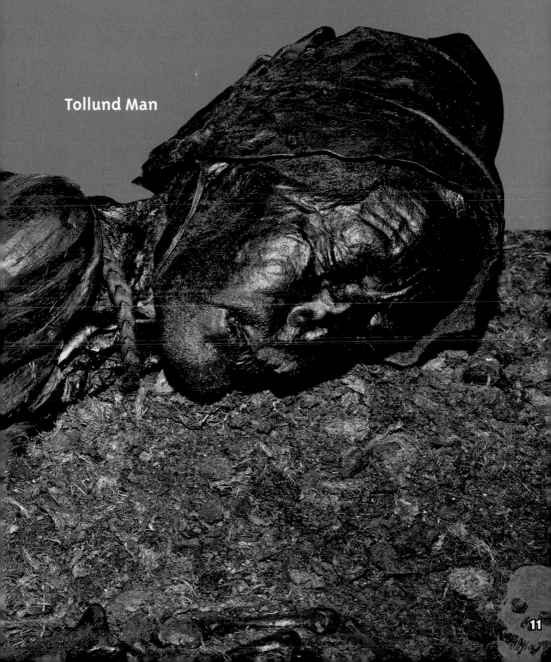

Tollund Man

Ötzi Man

In 1991, two hikers found a man frozen in the mountains between Italy and Austria. A 5,300-year-old murder mystery! The mummy, nicknamed Ötzi (OOT-zee), is one of the oldest mummies ever found.

He wears a cape and leather shoes. But when scientists took a closer look at Ötzi's body, they found a surprise. A stone arrowhead was stuck in his shoulder. Ötzi had been shot in the back! Who killed Ötzi over five thousand years ago and why? So far the case has gone cold!

Ötzi as he might have looked

Man-made Mummies

For thousands of years, people have made mummies. Many cultures believed that a person's spirit lives on after death.

WordWrap

CULTURE: A group of people who share beliefs and customs

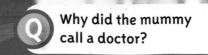
They thought spirits might need things in the next life. That's why mummies were sometimes buried with weapons, jewelry, food, or even mummies of favorite pets.

Different cultures had their own ways of making mummies. Some dried the bodies with sand or smoke. Others used chemicals to preserve bodies.

The first people to make mummies
may have been the Chinchorros.

Their mummies are 7,000 years old!
They are the oldest man-made
mummies ever found.

Tomb of Treasures

Ancient Egyptians made millions of mummies. In 1922, a scientist named Howard Carter found a special mummy in Egypt. Carter peeked into a dark tomb and was struck with amazement. Gold sparkled everywhere.

The Chinchorros mummified everyone who died, from babies to the oldest adults. They covered their mummies' faces with clay masks. Then the mummies were painted to make them black and shiny.

The culture disappeared around 3,000 years ago. These strange mummies were all that was left behind.

MUMMIFY: To treat a dead body so that it doesn't break down

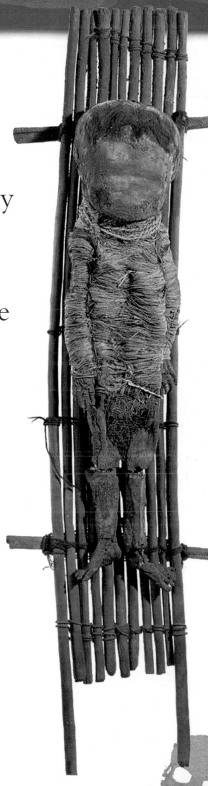

How to Make a Mummy

1

Workers remove organs such as the lungs and liver.

LUNGS   LIVERS

2

Mummy makers take out the brain through the nose with a large hook.

3

Workers wash the body and cover it with salts.

4

The body is left to dry for 40 days.

5

Workers rub scented oils on the mummy.

6

Workers wrap the mummy in linen.

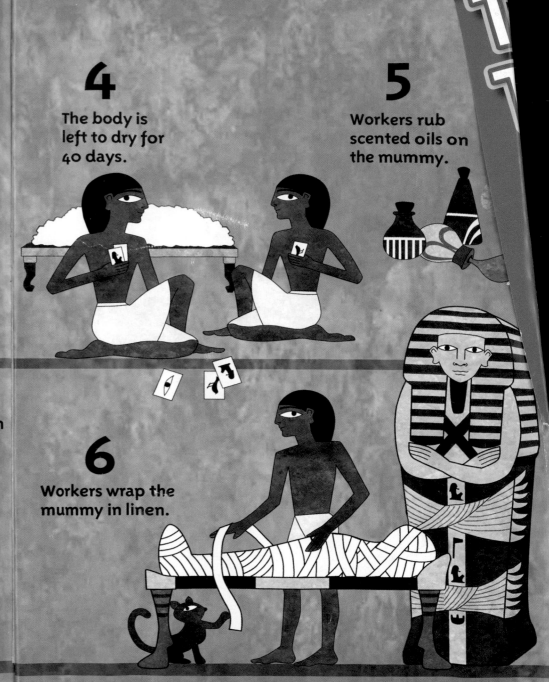

How to Make a Mummy

1

Workers remove organs such as the lungs and liver.

LUNGS   LIVERS

2

Mummy makers take out the brain through the nose with a large hook.

3

Workers wash the body and cover it with salts.

The Chinchorros mummified everyone who died, from babies to the oldest adults. They covered their mummies' faces with clay masks. Then the mummies were painted to make them black and shiny.

The culture disappeared around 3,000 years ago. These strange mummies were all that was left behind.

MUMMIFY: To treat a dead body so that it doesn't break down

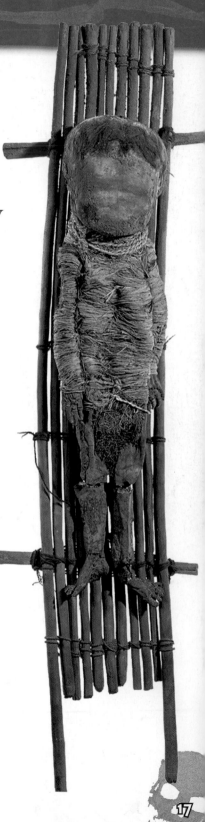

4

The body is
left to dry for
40 days.

5

Workers rub
scented oils on
the mummy.

6

Workers wrap the
mummy in linen.

Tomb of Treasures

Ancient Egyptians made millions of mummies. In 1922, a scientist named Howard Carter found a special mummy in Egypt. Carter peeked into a dark tomb and was struck with amazement. Gold sparkled everywhere.

Carter had found the
tomb of Tutankhamun
(toot–an–KAHM–uhn)!
Known as King Tut,
he died over 3,300
years ago. He was
only 18 years old.
But the young
king was buried with
priceless treasures.
Tut's tomb made
him the most
famous mummy
in the world.

TOMB: A grave,
room, or building for
holding a dead body

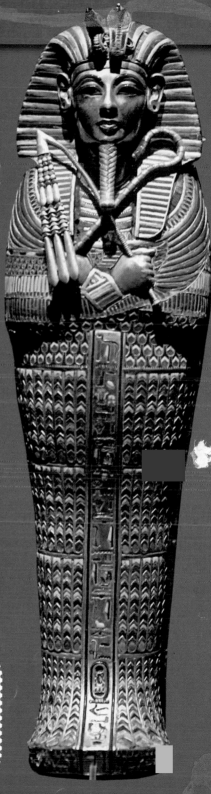

A Mummy's Curse

Howard Carter in the tomb
of King Tutankhamun

After the discovery of King Tut's tomb, people everywhere wanted to know more about the boy king. But not everything reported about Tut was true.

Shortly after the tomb was opened, one of Tut's discoverers died. Some people said that the boy king put a curse on the tomb.

Animal Wraps

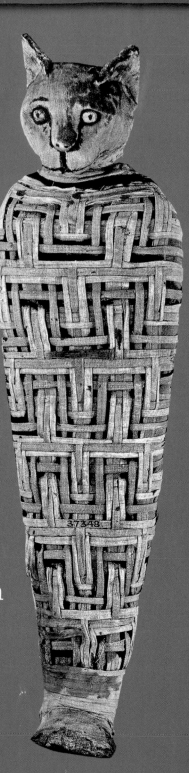

Ancient Egyptians didn't just make human mummies. They made many animal mummies too!

Favorite pets were sometimes mummified and buried with their owners. Egyptians thought cats were very special. Sometimes, when a cat died, the whole family would mourn its death.

Egyptians also made mummies of dogs, crocodiles, monkeys, and birds. These animals were believed to please the gods.

> MOURN: To feel or express sorrow or grief

Lovely Lady Mummy

Lady Dai may have looked like this.

Over 2,000 years ago, a wealthy Chinese woman known as Lady Dai died.

Her body was treated with salt. Salt takes water out of the body, which helps to keep it from rotting. The body was wrapped in 20 layers of silk.

Lady Dai was put into a nest of six beautifully painted coffins. Workers buried her at the bottom of a tunnel dug deep in the ground.

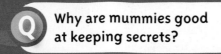
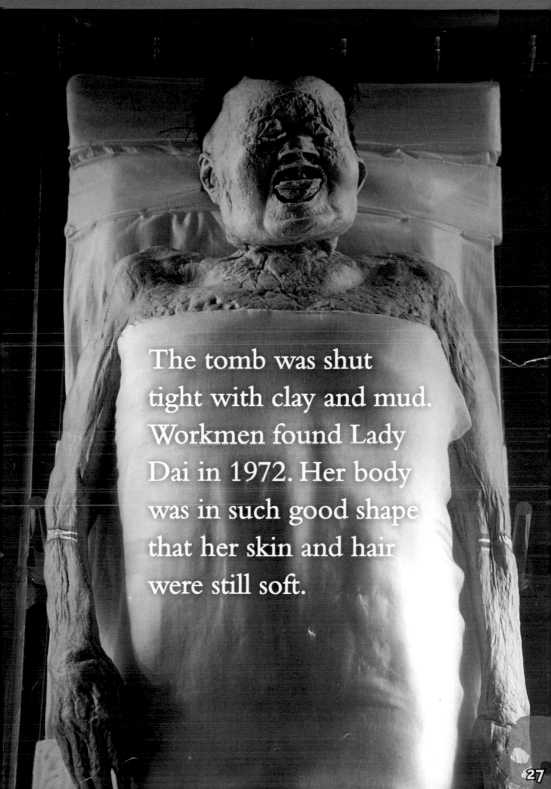

The tomb was shut tight with clay and mud. Workmen found Lady Dai in 1972. Her body was in such good shape that her skin and hair were still soft.

Mummies Today

Mummy-making is not just a thing of the ancient past. Some famous people have been mummified since then.

English thinker Jeremy Bentham died in 1832. He wanted his body to be used for science. Students took out his insides. They mummified his head. Then they dressed his skeleton in clothes. You can still go see him in England!

Secrets Unwrapped

Mummies can't talk. But they can still tell us many secrets about the past. Scientists study everything in and around a mummy's body.

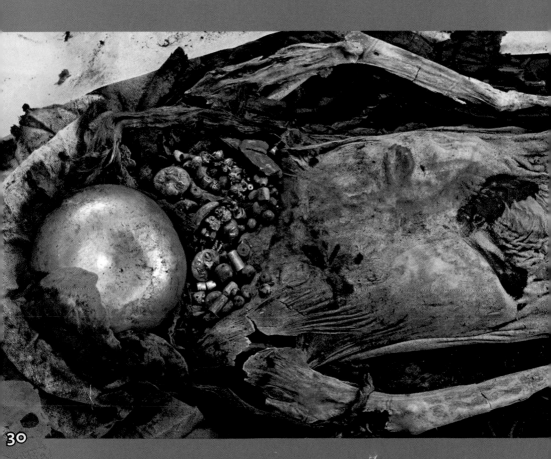

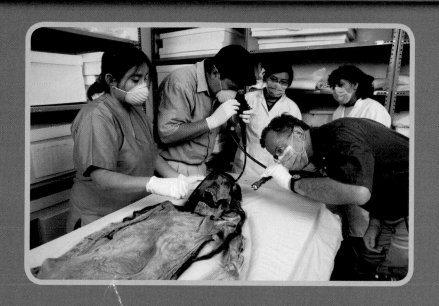

Food left in a mummy's stomach
tells about what people ate.
Broken bones tell about a person's life
and sometimes about his or her death.
Scientists can also examine a mummy's
clothes and the objects buried with it.

All hold clues to peoples'
religions and ways of life. In a way,
mummies are like time machines.

They give us a peek into the past.

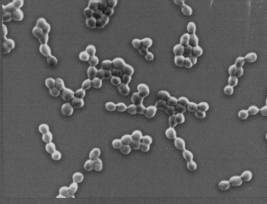

DECAY
To rot or break down

BACTERIA
Tiny living things that can only be seen through a microscope. Bacteria can cause human diseases.

BOGS
Swampy areas where special mosses grow. The plants make the area a tough place for bacteria to live.

TOMB
A grave, room, or building for holding a dead body

MUMMIFY
To treat a dead body so that it doesn't break down

CULTURE
A group of people who share beliefs and customs